SCREEN TIME AND CHILDREN

SCREEN TIME AND CHILDREN

AVERY NIGHTINGALE

CONTENTS

1 Introduction   1

2 Understanding Screen Time   3

3 Effects of Screen Time on Children   5

4 Setting Screen Time Limits   7

5 Choosing Age-Appropriate Content   9

6 Balancing Screen Time with Other Activities   11

7 Creating a Screen Time Schedule   13

8 Monitoring and Supervising Screen Time   15

9 Encouraging Healthy Screen Time Habits   17

10 Promoting Digital Well-being   19

11 Addressing Screen Time Challenges   21

12 Collaborating with Educators   23

13 Incorporating Screen Time in Education   25

14 Teaching Digital Citizenship   27

15 Supporting Parents in Managing Screen Time   29

16 Building Partnerships with Families   31

17 Providing Resources and Recommendations   33

18	Evaluating Screen Time Strategies	35
19	Research and Evidence-Based Practices	37
20	Professional Development for Educators	39
21	Assessing the Impact of Screen Time	41
22	Promoting Healthy Media Use	43
23	Understanding Online Safety	45
24	Fostering Positive Digital Experiences	47
25	Collaborating with Technology Companies	49
26	Developing Screen Time Policies	51
27	Advocating for Screen Time Guidelines	53
28	Engaging in Parent Education	55
29	Addressing Screen Time in School Policies	57
30	Promoting Screen-Free Activities	59
31	Conclusion	61

CHAPTER 1

Introduction

Screen time is the number of hours a person utilizes technology in many diverse formats, such as games, the internet, smartphones, tablets, television, films, the interactive and creating capacity, general and virtual events, simulations, digital television, etc. The uses of screens are fun interactive media for children and toddlers, and there are no specific guidelines. There is no doubt that many fascinating opportunities for the development of young children's growth are offered today by these kinds of interactions. Digital media can encourage much triumph over the physical and cognitive limits of the real world, which is difficult to match in the real world. Although the advantages of new technologies and interaction are evident, many concerns exist such as the potential risk of a sedentary lifestyle, possible negative relations with the well-being of individuals, couples, and children during parenting in the early years.

With the intention of providing perspectives from the family and the school on the use of digital tools and children's games, this code is proposed. This "Guide for parents and educators" has the virtue of recognizing the experimentation of concrete experiences in the ever-changing programming of digital tools and offers content and guidelines. This book offers "a selection experiment" to adults in the high interest and education sector for what you can do at a difficult historical moment. RAI, together with renowned experts in the field, has forged a tool to help parents in educational choices: psychologists, researchers, doctors, and professionals who closely monitor digital and IT news in order to give realistic advice. The aim is not to stigmatize the instruments but to invite everyone to reflect on the possible use of shared values and methods to make the most of the skills and attitudes that the technologies can encourage and enhance.

Understanding Screen Time

Interactions with screens have surpassed the definition of digital citizenship and literacy recommended by organizations like the International Society for Technology in Education (ISTE) and the National Association for Media Literacy Education (NAMLE). According to "The Loss of Children's Play through the Lens of Social Media," "overexposure to screens has profound effects on the way children learn, interact, and view the world." In this context, digital citizenship should imply a set of skills that prepares students to safely and responsibly access media content while also fostering critical thinking in order to analyze messages received on digital devices. Ideally, digital citizenship should become part of both K-12 practices and pedagogical practices, as recommended in the ISTE Standards for Students, Educators, and Coaches. In essence, digital citizenship is critical in guiding young children to appropriate and ethical practices.

In today's digital world, it is increasingly difficult to determine the right balance between the benefits and detriments of children's engagement with screens. The American Academy of Pediatrics (AAP) reports that children in the United States spend, on average, seven hours a day using screens. Overexposure to screens has negative effects on children's language and social skills, attention span, and sleep habits. Consequently, teachers and parents have an important role to play in creating healthy and developmentally supportive environments for children with diverse backgrounds and experiences. Less attention has been devoted to the study of short-term or long-term effects of the new digital literacy practices on the young children we are educating—both at home and school.

CHAPTER 3

Effects of Screen Time on Children

Professionals including the American Academy of Pediatrics have repeatedly expressed concerns that media use may interfere with the positive activities experienced by very young children, a period when the potential for media to interfere is greatest. For example, the time spent using screen media in children under the age of 3 was negatively related to the presence and quality of parental interactions. Others have also reported a negative relationship between screen media use and child-parent interactions for young children. It is thought that this diminished parent-child time may lead to missed opportunities to foster positive development.

Social and interactive TV watching is the most prevalent passive use of screen media. Each half-hour of television watched per day by preschoolers is associated with a 10% higher risk of having a parent-assessed attention problems. Also, when infants are exposed to background television, the researchers see decreases in quantity of language vocalizations, as well as a decrease in the duration they play with toys. Generation M2: Media in the Lives of 8- to 18-year-olds reported that by the time U.S. youth reached a median age of 12, they had spent almost 6 years of 24-hour days watching TV, playing video games, and using the computer (which can also include video watching).

Setting Screen Time Limits

In order to promote the child's active participation, media education, and interaction with available programs, applications, and games, it is positive that parents ensure the interaction of the child with their digital device. It is interesting to watch family programs or educational online activities along with the child because any parent interest is reflected in the student. It is important that the child is not only a passive receptor for media information but interprets it, questions, and expands their concepts. With constant interaction with the child, the brain develops and presents functional good results, since the pediatrician and scientist Daniel Becker, in an interview conducted by Nova Escola (2017), always "defended the excessive intellectual stimulation of children and referred to it as an investment in critical thinking".

How much is too much for my child? The first step in addressing these concerns is to set limits for your child's leisure screen time. Parents are often uncertain about how to balance the opportunities provided by digital media with the risks inherent in living in a media-saturated world. The American Academy of Pediatrics (AAP) recommends no recreational screen time for children younger than

18-24 months, and no more than one to two hours of high-quality content for children two years or older. These screen time guidelines from the American Academy of Pediatrics (AAP) also apply to use by adolescent caregivers at home, since without adult mediation and guidance, teens' media presence can be just as unproductive for their growth as it is for those who are younger.

CHAPTER 5

Choosing Age-Appropriate Content

The Palo Alto Medical Foundation's (2017) website provides a list of age-appropriate recommendations for children from preschool through teenage years and Beyond the Classroom's (2018) website also offers a list of educational apps for a variety of age groups. Beyond the Classroom, which provides learning centers for students after school, believes that educational apps can extend the learning for young children after school hours. These websites for experts provide guidance, but remember to take the time to research each app to meet the needs and interest of your individual child since every child is unique, and their experiences with these apps should be considered unique as well. All the studies lead to the importance of the co-viewing, where by watching the content with the child, parents can discuss what their children are watching, keep them safe and wise about the uses of digital technology, and also build stronger relationships with their children.

The review of apps, games, and videos can help parents make good choices for their children and their family circumstances. In the seventh edition of the JLPR, Uhls and Doty (2018) provide a "bounce card," a guide to which apps are the best ones for children.

The Interactive Media For Children (2017) website offers a tool to look by category or age level to find the best apps for children. Look at their apps database to find a variety of different kinds of apps. If you have a child, ask his or her teacher about age-appropriate apps that can help your child learn.

CHAPTER 6

Balancing Screen Time with Other Activities

The guidelines from the Canadian Society of Pediatrics recommend developing, promoting, and sustaining a balanced day across the education, health, and social systems. The new screen time guidelines are 'consistent with this goal'. Coined 'screen sense' via a visual partnership with the Canadian 24-Hour Movement Guidelines for Children and Youth, the digital behaviors comprise 3 items: screen education, sleep, and physical activity. After an introduction stating 'all we need to know' (i.e., video chatting with grandparents is positive for the baby; not 'screen time' but 'screen sense' understanding what are the key determinants influencing why, how much, what, and with whom children spend their time), the screen time subsection dares to outline the science informing the 1 hour upwards of sleep inversely related to screen time, 1 hour or less of recreational screen time, and approximately zero recreational screen time as of 24 months. Subsection recommendations and evidence for infants and toddlers (0-4 years), children (5-13 years), and youth (14-17 years) ends with: "Parents and educators play a key role in teaching children about healthy living, including safe and beneficial 'screen sense' behaviors.

Both the American Pediatrics Association and Canadian Society of Pediatrics have provided screen-time guidelines for a variety of different aspects of this topic. Given these guidelines, it is important to consider the research results from several meta-analyses and even more literature reviews on children (18 months-18 years) to determine the role of screen time on attention, executive functioning, and social development, the factors that are related to high screen use, and strategies to minimize the impact of high screen use. This is particularly important given that 1-1.5 hours of screen time for infants less than 18 months is now being recommended, a two-grade increase from the previous guideline.

CHAPTER 7

Creating a Screen Time Schedule

Use clock timers so children learn that technology use needs to be limited. Parents who don't use a timer are more likely to allow children to watch as much television as they want, since it may be a method of babysitting. This problem has been fixed with digital cable boxes that allow parents to impose limits on the amount of television their children can watch. Research has found that the ability to impose limits on television viewing directly reduces overweight. Such digital cable boxes also allow parents to block programming that's inappropriate for children. After doing this, it could be useful to talk to the children about how programming was blocked because its content would not be good for them to watch. This helps them understand that you will continue to use the control features of the digital cable box.

It is important to reduce excessive screen time by creating a schedule for technology use. For example, children can use technology within 20-minute episodes or the traditional 30-minute episodes when on a long trip. Make a technology schedule so children learn that technology use is important, but also limited. For example, you can allow them to use technology for 30 minutes a day only after they have done their homework, reading, and music practice for the day. Explain to them any presently observed behavior changes so they learn through experience that too much technology use is negatively influencing them.

CHAPTER 8

Monitoring and Supervising Screen Time

It's preferable to avoid television in the evening and for the child to watch programs at a certain hour. Television time should be monitored. If parents/educators decide to use a schedule, during the time of television, it is desirable to choose programs for the whole family. Regarding scheduled screen time activities, it is highly preferable that one of the programs in the chosen schedule is seen interactively with the family. During the two hours of screen time, children can choose schedules at different moments of the weekend: morning, evening, and afternoon. This will give the child the opportunity to be able to see different programs. If one of the schedules is especially long, like a movie, they should decide if they would like to watch anything else during the two hours of screen time. It is best to avoid exceeding the recommended 14 hours of screen time for ages 3-4 and 18 hours for ages 5-18.

Moderation, good judgment, and some easy-to-follow guidelines can solve most of the problems. Parents and educators can set clear rules about screen time and be consistent and firm with these guidelines. Parents and educators can create a list of what screen entertainment is allowed and when it is allowed. For example, in many homes, a recommendation is that there is no television during the week. The child may watch television only in the morning on Saturday and Sunday. In addition, they may select another 2 hours of screen time during weekends, normally on Saturday and Sunday afternoons.

CHAPTER 9

Encouraging Healthy Screen Time Habits

According to the American Academy of Pediatrics (AAP) screen time and children recommendations, children below two should have no screen time at all, and in the older age groups, the (quality) screen time should be conducted judiciously. In reality, though, implementing these guidelines is pretty challenging, even for the most well-intentioned parents. Here are some options to contemplate, which aren't necessarily rocket science, but phenomenally mattering. None of the options accommodate the "out of sight, out of mind" ethos. You surely would have seen that kids are the experts at finding long-lost articles. They explore even when the item isn't there where they left it—on the living room couch or on the bedroom nightstand. Same goes for screens, especially when you hide gadgets to reclaim some peace at home. If you don't want your kids to start missing their cherished adventures with screens in their life, while curiously pursuing them, or experimenting with the dangers of randomly pushing buttons on their parents' gadget, it's your best bet to keep the screens within sight. You need to set the limit, more than once, and to stick to it religiously. Humans (irrespective of age) like constraints as long as they can "see the walls" of the limitations, and you should be very assertive about reminding them of what it means to cross these walls. Even though undue penalties or excessive policing is counterproductive for kids belonging to the tunnel of screen time hell, they should quickly understand the implications of not sticking to the limit.

Screen time for kids is an oft-contested topic. There are a myriad of want-to-be-the-best parents out there who have unhealthy obsessions with keeping electronics out of kids' hands—forcing them onto an old-school, paleolithic track. And then there are parents who are blissfully, blindly ignorant about the dangers of the technological exposure to their kids. After all, technology-based education is a huge thing these days. The truth, as always, seems to lie somewhere in between the opposing extremes. If you are an academician reading this, I am pretty sure you are doing quite well at maintaining a balance—probably by virtue of your deep, ongoing intimacy with scientific literature. But if you are a non-academician and a parent, how do you decide what the healthy screen time balance looks like in order to avoid the negative repercussions? Is it even within grasp anymore?

CHAPTER 10

Promoting Digital Well-being

Guidelines continually offer recommendations to restrict and reduce the time children spend with digital devices. A 2016 recommendation of the American Academy of Pediatrics (AAP) recommended that for children aged 2-5, parental co-viewing is a necessity for making the most of media, and children aged 6 and older acquire a total of 1-2 hours of high-quality programs per day. The 2018 version removed the limit of screen time and replaced it with the goal of "balancing media activities with other healthy behaviors." The tone of the recommendation implies that screen time is unhealthy with only a few types of media potentially acceptable. For example, one media effort to capture the spirit of the new guideline is National Public Radio's Health Blog "In New Guidelines, the AIDS the Limit Screen Time for Children." Circulating messages about limiting media use fails to recognize the potential benefits of some forms of media for children and fails to address the many ways in which media use is a part of contemporary children's lives. If children use devices responsibly, the relationship between screen time and negative outcomes is relatively small. At a time when media comprises a significant part of family routines and children's lives, it would be a disservice to parents to simply limit their children's use without acknowledging and supporting more sophisticated and nuanced digital parenting.

Excessive digital use is associated with a range of negative physical and mental health outcomes for children, including lower levels of overall happiness, unhappiness with life, psychosocial health (e.g., acting as though not fully alive, not active and energized, feeling low), higher levels of anxiety, sleep disturbances, and depression. Associations between screen time and other potential outcomes, such as aggression, conduct problems, and poorer academic performance, are less consistent. Yet, it is unknown whether excessive digital use causes these associations. Longitudinal research studies are needed to understand whether detrimental outcomes are the result of excessive digital use or whether children at higher risk for these outcomes are more likely to engage in excessive use.

CHAPTER 11

Addressing Screen Time Challenges

Given the critical role of early learning in later school success and longer-term developmental trajectories, it is crucial for educators to understand their role in supporting children's healthy development in the digital age. Policymakers should allocate resources for both research and the development and testing of educational and clinical tools. Clinical tools include those for enhancing family functions (i.e., promoting positive parent-child interactions and reducing conflict so families have opportunities for play, reading, and family conversation), as well as methods for gauging readiness of children and families for technology, setting expectations for use, and those that screen and modify digital overuse symptoms by promoting healthy activities and skills. Solutions should consider different learning goals and developmentally appropriate practice and should be designed to minimize inequalities.

Because screen reliance can create challenges for families, educators, and policymakers, it is important to be thoughtful about the use of technology with children. When observed, overuse of technology (increased screen time and dependence on screens for managing experiences) may be an indication that there are other underlying issues. These include high levels of family conflict and less attuned parenting, sensitive parenting, and learning activities. In the long run, these issues may become detrimental for child development and functioning. It is important to use tools to diagnose and address these challenges. Educators should receive more extensive training and support for how to diagnose and guide parents with tools to screen for both technology overuse and related parenting challenges. Adaptation and testing of tools for specific populations and community needs are encouraged.

CHAPTER 12

Collaborating with Educators

The key question for educational purposes appears to be when, to which children, under what conditions, and for which outcomes are the technologies beneficial. Some findings suggest that technology serves young learners' cognitive growth, helps teach concepts and higher cognitive functions, may stimulate pre-readers, offers opportunities for scientific reasoning, encourages negotiations, and engages in dialogues around mathematics, and helps learners adjust to differences in possible solutions to problems. More agreement exists for the idea that more studies have to be conducted focusing on children's interaction with technologies.

By contrast, the National Association for the Education of Young Children and the Fred Rogers Center for Early Learning and Children's Media at St. Vincent College in Latrobe in 2012 released a joint Position Statement on Technology and Interactive Media as Tools in Early Childhood Programs, arguing that:

Educators often observe children in settings away from home, and their insights can help round out parents' understanding of children's screen use. Schools often use computers in settings or for curricular requirements, yet the nature of such use is only recently studied. In 2015, the American Academy of Pediatrics and the Children's Hospital Association recommended against screen time in child care settings for children 2 years of age and younger. These recommendations recognize that although screen time can be educational and entertaining, it may displace time spent with other nurturing activities or interactions.

CHAPTER 13

Incorporating Screen Time in Education

Anecdotally, one may see the heavy usage of smart devices by children from distressed families as well, and other related elements may, in fact, be beneficial to the children in ways that affluent parents are not able to currently or are resistant in identifying the potential positive advantages that technology can bring to children when its usage is appropriately mediated, monitored, and made purposeful. Poverty is not an indicator of disability. However, children from distressed families are at higher risk of having poor physical and mental health. They also may be more likely to have bigger problems in other areas, which include social and emotional well-being and educational performance. Cognitive abilities grow at the fastest pace during the early years. It involves not only learning facts but learning how to use such facts. The education received during this period is crucial as those years set the stage for progression throughout life.

Formal instruction at a young age is limited for those who do not have access to preschool or ECE (early childhood education) programs and are not able to learn through family education at home. Early disadvantage can have a lasting impact, as evidence shows that high-quality preschool can lead to significant improvements in learning scores that can be recognized and built upon over time. Advancements in technology can potentially offer solutions to such problems by making education more accessible, especially to those who live in remote locations where high-quality schools or children's books may not be easily accessible. The integration of technology in education amplifies the typically occurring inter-group disparities. Most of the education technology and apps resonate the privileged experience of those who are either affluent or those who live in the developed world.

CHAPTER 14

Teaching Digital Citizenship

These guidelines are compatible with others and can be adapted to shape activities. Children should be expected to demonstrate the four qualities of digital citizenship when communicating, publishing information, or participating in digital media activities at home: Demonstrating safe and appropriate online behavior. Protecting private/personal information and managing digital identity. Protecting digital reputation. Plagiarism, cyberbullying, and privacy violations can carry real-world consequences. Discuss digital citizenship with your child's teacher and technology coordinator, and offer support by making suggestions or providing tools for the classroom. Provide clear information to your school's administration if you encounter new commercial tools or walled gardens, and advocate for free, secure, and interoperable tools that can be independently accessed and used by all parents and students.

So many families struggle with screen-time rules because their kids have joined a digital world that is largely invisible to the adults who care about them. Parents rightly feel that they need to be responsible digital citizens and model respect and kindness online. The lines between offline and online friendships and relationships are more blurred than ever, and because there is no such thing as two separate non-interacting worlds anymore, there is no such thing as mindfully unplugging or giving a child two hours of technology time the same week we teach community outreach. Digital citizens acknowledge these challenges and work with them. If policing and protecting your child worked, then technology use would not be such a pervasive conflict.

CHAPTER 15

Supporting Parents in Managing Screen Time

Unfortunately, research indicates that many parents are not well informed about how their children spend time with media. Further, evidence from nationally representative household surveys suggests that many parents do not know of the media guidelines provided by the AAP. Educational campaigns and technological innovation can address some of the challenges associated with the use of screen time in the home. This chapter outlines opportunities for promoting best practices among parents and children by encouraging children to visit educational websites, playing together with children using new digital tools, leveraging digital resources to foster children's academic engagement and reduce the school readiness gap, preparing children for the increasingly connected world that we live in and designing technological interventions that support caregivers in setting appropriate limits on children's screen time.

The AAP recommends that positive parenting practices (such as setting appropriate limits for children) be encouraged in the development of a healthy media diet. Technology can play a key role in supporting parents' efforts to manage children's screen time. Parents are in a unique position to serve as role models for their children.

Showing children how to act in the physical world and the online world is equally important. Parents are encouraged to join children in game playing, ensure their children are good online citizens, and help protect them from cyberbullies and scams.

CHAPTER 16

Building Partnerships with Families

In order to support young children's health and well-being, screen time should replace time spent in active play, self-care routines, reading, resting, and conversing with others. Health care providers and early educators should support parents in selecting and using appropriate and beneficial media, information, and programs. Early learning practitioners should serve as partners with families and other health care providers to engage in regular two-way, goal-oriented and open communication. Families who collaborate and communicate effectively with early learning programs and teachers help children to feel secure and valued while progressing in nurturing environments.

Create a positive and welcoming environment for all parent members. All families are encouraged to participate in decision-making and governance; i.e., joining a parent advisory committee, attending family events, or occasional meetings with a parent and child specialist or early education programs. Children always receive the same warm welcome and levels of respect when they are enrolled and their families are actively included in the educational process. Parent and family contact information is regularly assessed to ensure the effectiveness of communication with early childhood educators. Early learning center policies are well-aligned in order to make 'family schedules' less aggressive and provide families with opportunities to volunteer or participate in other ways in their children's learning.

Research on early learning environments highlights the important contributions of families and early childhood educators. Teachers who demonstrate respectful and competent behaviors while forming secure relationships with parents and children will be viewed as experienced, knowledgeable, valuable, and caring. In fact, when parenting and early childhood educators are genuinely and equally involved, parents, educators, and young children benefit.

CHAPTER 17

Providing Resources and Recommendations

To develop these guidelines, I synthesized advice learned from the experts who guide screen time for their own children with advice from pediatricians and educators. I also used a variety of search engines, such as Google Scholar, as well as a digital summary of 6000 of the most important articles in the scientific literature produced in one year. These 6000 were logged and categorized by reviewers according to their relevance for the range of 16 age levels that distinguish the stages of brain development and cognitive learning where the role of screen exposure is most critical. I analyzed available resources, such as the reports and guidance articles produced by the American Academy of Pediatrics or the World Health Organization.

When I embarked on this work, my goal was not merely to do a content analysis, but to synthesize clear and coherent guidelines for preventing or mitigating the most pernicious outcomes noted in the research. Many of these outcomes are not just theoretical risks, but real threats to human thriving and survival. Accordingly, I offer to parents, educators, caregivers, medical professionals, librarians, policy-makers, game-designers, app-developers, and the general public two documents: one with broad guidelines applicable across multiple contexts, and the other with resources and specific recommendations for 16 different age ranges (0-8) across four contexts: at home, in libraries and schools, in medical settings, and during play.

CHAPTER 18

Evaluating Screen Time Strategies

In order to truly fix these lapses, however, we need appropriate measures for screen time self-reports. Much in the same way that self-reports of recall for the amount of food consumed on a specific day can be modeled using plausible foods and portions, a similar approach can be taken for screen time. Some measures also provide descriptors for "mindless" vs. "enjoyable" vs. "meaningful" screen time. With truly sensitive and specific measurements, screen time may soon become as amenable to self-regulation as credit card debt, snacking habits, or even leisure time. Imagine using smartphone data to examine in-the-moment characteristics of screen time just as early eating time or stress eating are being examined at long last.

Finally, there should be some critical questions asked concerning the wisdom of future return connections between general childrearing initiatives and screen time. The ubiquitous and continual nature of this particular environmental true measure almost demand that we do so. Elements like aloud reading or frequent meals should avoid most of these concerns. In comparison, it is likely that the long-run impact of cultural shifts in screen use may differ greatly between age groups and, conceivably, between high- and low-risk groups as well as minority vs. majority culture. Though universalistic education principles should apply to potential concerns, it is always intellectually useful to brainstorm "might the tide work differently for adolescents?"

CHAPTER 19

Research and Evidence-Based Practices

The advent of portable media players and the dramatic increase in diffusion of smartphones have led to easier access to electronic media. Although the use of electronic media devices by children to consume various types of content has become increasingly common, little is known about their long-term usage patterns or impact on child development. Despite the extensive amount of time children spend using electronic media each day, few medical or public health interventions based on child development research findings exist to guide clinical practice. Future interventions can use evidence-based principles, outlined below, aimed at promoting the role of e-media in fostering rather than hindering enriched, supportive, and diverse language environments in which parent/child interactions are paramount.

The prevalence and risks associated with excessive use of electronic media warrant a better understanding of the contributing factors and their impact. It showed that nearly all U.S. children 8–18 years of age reported at least occasional use of video games (97%, 95% confidence interval [CI] = 96% to 98%), or computers (97%), and more than three-quarters reported using video games (79%) or computers (81%) in the past month. Watching television was, by far, the most common activity for this age group, with 93% of children reporting this use in the past month. Adolescents (14–18 years of age) both watched television and used computers significantly more often than younger children (8–13 years of age). Adolescents also reported increased use of more types of screens, including cell-phone video games, portable video players, and tablets.

CHAPTER 20

Professional Development for Educators

Because various applications of tablets and interactive e-books for young children are in their early stage of discussions for professionals in the field of early childhood education, some educators may not fully understand or appreciate the differences between the linear informational orientation of traditional educational television programs and the interactive instructional designs of "educational" apps. One possible way to review available apps may be using a series of original Rubric for Reviewing Apps. There are many good and useful commercial apps for young children that can allow them to access previously unavailable or unattainable information or professional knowledge about the external world, including encyclopedic information or self-help books. All people have limited time and there are only 24 hours a day (only 16 hours while awake) for any individuals. To make sure this value of limited time is under rigorous balance, however, the purpose of spending time on app use should be clear to any adults who want to support young children's healthy intellectual development efficiently through outdoor activities for movement, writing, exercises, game plays, and some hobbies, bath and bed times, meals, and social events.

After offering guidelines for parents to encourage and support healthy media use by young children, guidelines for educators are offered. To minimize the screen time for young children during early childhood, it should not be an exaggerated substitute for direct human contact with peers, teachers, and caregivers who are known to promote intellectual and socio-emotional development during early childhood more forcefully than any media or technology resource. It should also be emphasized that even the most popular and powerful screens, such as educational and non-educational TV programs and tablet computers, do not offer a new foreign language-like experience during the critical period for learning a first language when human beings use only sense perceptions to learn their first language.

CHAPTER 21

Assessing the Impact of Screen Time

There are substantial differences in how television viewing is related to children's academic achievement as a function of children's sex, race, economic status, and category of program viewing, as well as children growing up in mothers with different educational levels. Beyond these purely demographic variables, it is clear that different experiences vary in their impact as functions of child characteristics. A key child characteristic is the child's cognitive maturity. Cognitive maturity has a substantial effect on both the ability to learn from educational television, as well as on its overall impact. Early educational television viewing promoting language development is related to readiness for primary education and overall school achievement, only if preschoolers also eat breakfast with their parents, are read to often, and belong to an intact family. However, for children 6-9 years of age, time watching educational television is related to improved reading, with no moderator variables.

There are fundamental issues associated with most research into screen time, if for no other reason than that "screen time" is such a broad term that in itself it is virtually meaningless. Different types of screen use - educational versus purely entertaining; different screen devices (TV, computer, and mobile phone); and different implementations (e.g., playing an educational game online versus watching YouTube versus tweeting versus reading) - are virtually endless. provide a literature review of the research documenting children's use of mobile devices from 1997 up to 2013, and its impact on development, across areas such as physical development, social interactive development, language development, cognitive development, and psychosocial development.

CHAPTER 22

Promoting Healthy Media Use

Research indicates that children's brains and bodies get optimal benefits from digital media when:

Screen time isn't the dominant activity - 90 minutes or less a day is about right so children can make time for reading, playing, creating, and spending time with family and friends. Media is high-quality - Focus on how children engage with digital media instead of the kind or time children spend with media. Some programs and media can help children learn how to express emotion, increase imagination, and set a foundation for learning. Discuss content with children, not their interactions or experiences. Time is shared - Encourage families and friends to participate in digital media with children for connection, fun, and learning. Shared experiences can help ensure learning about social, emotional, and physical development for children. Set screen time when to go on or turn off based on the daily routine and schedules for children. Digital media is there to strengthen learning in the real world, not replace it - Design careful integration between digital technology and experiences in nurturing and children's learning. Digital media can be used for extending development and learning. For that to happen, there should be guided screen viewing, off-screen joint-attention experiences and debriefing discussions and conversations. Encourage children to ask question(s) and figure out whether or not children find their answers to be interesting and satisfactory. Review and discuss with children what they like and what they can learn from the digital media content and its appeal. Assist children in evaluating and making safe and empowering progress in experiences whenever possible, trusted adult support is there.

CHAPTER 23

Understanding Online Safety

But we also need to make some decisions around technology when it comes to our children's safety and digital habits: Parents ask me all the time what the "right time" is to finally get a smartphone for their child. The short answer is that there is no "right time". There is only the right time for you. We cannot expect children to know what is safe, appropriate, or good for them if our expectations of their behaviors are not, in fact, backed up by any rules or boundaries. I often encourage parents to create a family media agreement which outlines what is and is not allowed, what the rules are around certain sites and how much time is allowed for different activities. Setting these rules out with children has been shown to be so much more effective in helping to shape a child researching to the levels of the brain where they're fully able to process and understand by 21.

Children are just learning about this incredible digital world in which we all live. We cannot expect them to know the rules for being safe at all times – or for them to know what is and what is not appropriate. Let's teach them. Better yet, let's empower them with the confidence they need to navigate social media safely on their own.

Better yet, let's get them to the point at which they are even asking permission to try anything out online – because they now understand how they can stay safe, how to spot content that is not appropriate, or would not make their parents proud - and have a conversational relationship open enough with you for them to be making the kind of judgment that earns them a 'yes'. We also need to work with our children to help them understand some of the things that might prompt them to keep secrets from us and to not want to talk about social media incidents they are involved in.

CHAPTER 24

Fostering Positive Digital Experiences

Positive Digital Experiences (PDE) are created through the quality use of technology, including digitally mediated facilitation. In higher grades where students have almost steady access to technology, you can use it to enable voice, choice, and agency. As an instructor, I sometimes assume that students already know how to be proactive in the use of the devices that surround us. But children need our help to get there. Try talking with your students about several strategies used to help digital conversations through media creation and curation, as well as techniques they can employ to identify reliable sources when seeking to research and elevate discussions online.

As adults, we often find ourselves lamenting "the good old days" while we watch our kids spend hours online, posting and sharing. The truth is, connections made online can become just as deep, meaningful, and impactful as those made in person. It's permitted for us to challenge this new being, but we must also acknowledge that, like the ones before them, our children are making new connections - what we characterize as vital online conversations. Given that these new connections have become essential, it's incumbent upon us to figure out ways to guide conversations amongst and between students and teenagers about putting together useful posts, most exciting surprising consequences, or advocating against digital injustices.

CHAPTER 25

Collaborating with Technology Companies

There is a lot of evidence on what works when used well. Capitalizing on it requires trust, communication, and synthesis. We hope the guidelines presented in this article serve as a catalyst, rather than as a culminating effort, addressing our primary concern of having generations grow up knowing how much and when technology is beneficial and when it is clearly not. Creating such a future involves the collaboration of parents, educators, designers, children, and everyone involved with them. We acknowledge the difficulty in synchronizing collaborations among such vested, but disparate, groups, but we are hopeful that the ever-increasing, globally connected communication infrastructure that is currently at our fingertips will bring us closer to that future. We also hope that, rather than ending the conversation, this article serves to present some of the initial issues in parenting and teaching using technology to a larger cross-section of society, including researchers from fields beyond the cognitive sciences, so that they can bring additional knowledge and perspective to the table.

We invite technology developers to collaborate with researchers and educators. Together, these communities can improve our understanding of the amount and type of parenting and teaching that technology-enhanced learning requires. Developers can share usage data and provide knowledge of how their technology works. This can include what features are most effective and with what game mechanics they engage players, engage them deeply, and for the long term. Both sides can collaborate to create dashboards for parents and teachers with features that track children's use and display indicators of progress in learning. Sharing the data and developing the dashboards is the easy and passive part. Collaboration on how best to use those tools is an act of co-location. A continuation will involve collaboration communication on what works or doesn't work for different children and under what context. This can be accomplished with online portals for crowdsourcing this information through technology-facilitated communication.

CHAPTER 26

Developing Screen Time Policies

For example, because daily use of digital media is the reality for most children and families, NAEYC and the Fred Rogers Center suggest screen time policies that require at least some positive screen experiences in early childhood programs to help children develop both challenging and nourishing relationships with media. In addition to (or in lieu of) a particular list of approved programs or online services, the Judy Center in Baltimore requires that young children experience "quality educational media and technology that support a rich learning environment" (p.1). A Screen Time Policy must also be open to interpretation based on responsive approaches to meeting children's unique developmental needs and interests, recognizing the diversity and differences in programs. According to the National Association for the Education of Young Children (NAEYC), policies should be shared and revised through open communication with everyone involved in the process of educating young children.

The National Association for the Education of Young Children (NAEYC) and the Fred Rogers Center caution educators to avoid banning digital media because - whether educators like it or not - digital media have a growing presence in the lives of children, families, and society at large (as numerous examples in the earlier question demonstrate). What educators can control is the quality and quantity of the media they use in their programs. To that end, NAEYC and the Fred Rogers Center recommend educators develop or revise written screen time policies to help provide "consistent, less confusing messages to families about the role of technology in high-quality programs for young children" (NAEYC & Fred Rogers Center, 2012, p. 14).

CHAPTER 27

Advocating for Screen Time Guidelines

The purpose of this paper is not to build new screen time guidelines for public consumption. Instead, it is a call to modify the public forum of media literacy to our community and make citizens aware of potential pitfalls and erroneous research-based guidelines. As researchers of screen time and developing computer mass communication and multimedia systems, we write this paper to reflect upon existing guidance in the domain – primarily recommendations that emerged from the National Association for the Education of Young Children and the Fred Rogers Center – and to elicit advice that these reflections may offer for public stakeholders.

Concern over excessive screen time is warranted, and researchers are eager to understand and create screen time guidelines that promote and protect children's development, learning, and well-being. Despite all the research that suggests risk factors that contribute to negative screen time outcomes for children, no research base currently exists to create definitive screen time guidelines for public dissemination. Yet, industry and experts proceed as if evidence-based recommendations are available. Popular press articles offer advice about screen time that may not reflect actual screen time recommendations based on high-quality research. Revisions have appeared from the American Academy of Pediatrics. Experience-based minimalist guidelines have also been developed by Stanford University pediatricians Cris Rowan and Betsy Bitner, and by many others. Other evidence-based guidelines could reasonably emerge as scientists orchestrate and create high-quality research on screen time for children.